CHRONICLES OF UQ
EPISODE 6
Synchronic Intelligences

Dedication:

To my beloved children, Mario (Teik), Bruna, Victor, and Bárbara, and to my dear Sansa&Cia, who are the inspiration and reason behind my relentless pursuit of knowledge. You are my strength and motivation to share my ideas and experiences.

To my husband José de Vasconcelos Filho, whose collaboration and support were crucial in the creation of this book. Your unwavering dedication and support are a precious gift in my life.

To my dear grandchildren, Davi, Vivi, and João Gabriel, who represent the continuity of our stories and the hope for a bright future. May this book inspire you to explore your passions and seek truth in all things.

To my sons-in-law, daughters-in-law, and friends, Nikolas Bucvar, Eduardo, Jana, and Jacque, who strengthen our family with their love, support, and valuable contributions. I am grateful for being part of this journey and for sharing your enriching perspectives and experiences.

May it be dedicated to all of you, my beloved family, with all my love and gratitude.

Katia Doria da Fonseca Vasconcelos

INTRODUCTION

Welcome to the Chronicles of UQ - Episode 6: Synchronic Intelligences! In this work, we will explore the practical application of the UQ concept (Universal Synchronic Intelligence Quotient) and demonstrate how lateral thinking can be used as a powerful tool to solve complex problems.

Unlike the conventional everyday cases, which are often boring and trapped in an exhausting reality, we have chosen to create a different story to illustrate the potential of UQ in practice. Through the Chronicles of UQ, we will present fictional cases that challenge your way of thinking and allow you to explore new possibilities.

To support our approach, we consider relevant case studies and scientific research. Researchers at Stanford University, for example, have shown that the development of resilience and emotional control increases the likelihood of achieving positive outcomes in careers and relationships. Clayton Christensen, a renowned professor of Business Administration at Harvard, emphasizes that disruptive innovation requires a change in approach and overcoming outdated paradigms.

Additionally, we highlight the work of Daniel Kahneman, a psychologist and Nobel laureate economist, who reminds us that our decisions are influenced by how we perceive problems. By adopting a positive perspective and viewing challenges as learning opportunities, we can make wiser decisions and achieve superior results.

The theory of emotional intelligence, developed by Daniel Goleman, is also aligned with the concept of UQ. It emphasizes the importance of emotional balance for personal and professional success. Howard Gardner, a renowned psychologist and professor at the Harvard Graduate School of Education, emphasizes the importance of balancing and developing all our intelligences, going beyond logical-mathematical intelligence.

Based on these references and other advocates of innovative thinking, we reinforce the importance of adopting a new perspective in the face of problems. By balancing our potentials through 360-degree vision, resilience, adaptability, synchronicity, and emotional control, we will be prepared to face challenges with confidence, creativity, and effectiveness.

In the Chronicles of UQ, our goal is to exemplify how this concept can be adopted in practice. Through fictional stories, we will follow the adventures of characters like Arqueu, Psiqueu, Diana, Malashi, and Ikara. Facing challenging situations, they will inspire us to adopt a more balanced approach, seeing problems as opportunities for learning and personal growth.

Furthermore, by exploring the Chronicles of UQ, we will be challenged to think laterally, expanding our creativity and connecting ideas in innovative ways. These stories invite us to explore new paths and expand the boundaries of conventional thinking, allowing us to develop innovative solutions and see beyond the limits of the ordinary.

So, get ready to immerse yourself in a world of imagination, reflection, and epic adventures. The Chronicles of UQ - Episode 6: Synchronic Intelligences are ready to guide you on an exciting journey in search of the transformative power of the convergence of ideals. Discover how the UQ concept can be applied in practice and embrace the challenge of forging a path to a brighter future.

TABLE OF CONTENTS

The Chronicles of UQ - Episode 6: Synchronic Intelligences invite you, our reader, to immerse yourself in a world of imagination, reflection, and epic adventures. This series of fictional stories seeks to provide an opportunity for us to develop the power of 360-degree vision within the context of lateral thinking and expand our creativity. Through the pages of these chronicles, we are challenged to explore new paths, connect ideas, and push the boundaries of conventional thinking, strengthening our ability to find innovative solutions and see beyond the limits of the ordinary.

Since the first episode, hidden clues have been scattered throughout the narrative, awaiting a keen detective like yourself. Here is the challenge: piece together the puzzle of this intricate plot, deciphering the enigmas woven between the lines. Each page contains encoded secrets, waiting for a curious mind to unravel them.

In the previous episodes, we witnessed the incredible journey of Diana, Arqueu, Psiqueu, Malashi, Ikara, and the great council of universe-protecting gods. Together, they played a crucial role in the reconstruction of Earth, forgiving Malashi for their past actions and creating a new world of unparalleled beauty. This new Earth housed species from all planets, a true amalgamation of generously donated life.

However, an unexpected reunion shook the foundations of this newly achieved harmony. Malashi encountered their former love, Kaisa, but realized that her escape to the

Earth of Kerus, simulating her own death, was a sign that they were no longer connected in the same way. This profound rupture led Kaisa to make a terrible decision for the future of Earth, unbalancing its UQ potentials.

Driven by pain and anger, Kaisa diverted an asteroid from its trajectory, directing it on a collision course with Earth, causing the extinction we now know as the end of the dinosaur era. Our heroes faced this immense challenge, but what tragic fate awaited them?

To answer this crucial question, we invite you to dive into the following pages, where clues have deliberately been left throughout the series. Each page holds hidden secrets that will challenge you to decipher a complex enigma. Remember that this series is not just a fictional story but also an exercise in exploring our own potentials and how to balance them using the key of UQ.

Be prepared for a journey full of mysteries and discoveries as we gradually unveil the clues that lead to the ultimate solution. At the end of this episode, we will reveal the key to decoding the puzzle. Stay alert and enjoy the thrilling journey that lies ahead.

Now, get ready to explore a world of imagination, reflection, and epic adventures. The Chronicles of UQ - Episode 6: Synchronic Intelligences await you, inviting you to explore the transformative power of converging ideals and embrace the great challenge of understanding how your path to a brighter future will unfold from here on.

CHAPTER 1 FROM ZERO TO ONE

In the midst of a softly illuminated room, with curtains filtering the faint light of the Pleiades, a large table occupied the center of the space. Upon it, a myriad of documents and papers filled with detailed notes portrayed the arduous task before the present authorities. Imposing figures from different worlds and dimensions sat around the table, engrossed in heated discussions about the future of Earth following the devastating asteroid impact that wiped out the dinosaurs and a large portion of the planet.

In this solemn environment, filled with murmurs and tension, the air was charged with anticipation. The most notable and influential personalities, representing diverse peoples and civilizations, gathered with an unexpected solution, eager to reveal to everyone the formula they had discovered for the recovery and preservation of planet Earth. The planet had suffered its third attack, the most recent being the asteroid's overwhelming power that caused the demise of the dinosaurs.

While the room echoed with the energetic voices and passionate arguments of the authorities, an unquestionable figure entered the chamber. Shangai, the supreme leader of the Council of Protector Gods of the Universes, walked calmly and confidently towards Cerus, the leader responsible for the great discovery, who was about to speak.

Facing a panel magnificently adorned with engravings and images of the heroes Malashi, Psiqueu, Arqueu, Diana, and Ikara, Shangai and Cerus approached, examining every detail with discerning eyes. Discreet whispers echoed between them as they contemplated the depictions of the fearless saviors of Earth.

Finally, Cerus announced to those present that their commission of genetic engineers would recreate, using the genetic material collected from Malashi, Ikara, Diana, Psiqueu, and Arqueu, a being that would restart the human species, to inhabit and develop on planet Earth. In doing so, they would harness the qualities of our heroes for this purpose, as within them lay all the necessary characteristics for the beginning of a more prepared civilization, ready to survive and develop in a more perfect and adaptable manner to the planet.

"From Malashi, we will utilize the genetic part that represents their unwavering resilience. From Psiqueu, we will harness the potential of their transcendental emotional control, depicting the inner strength they carry in battles fought to protect humanity. From Arqueu, we will make use of their 360-degree vision and expanded perception, personifying the wisdom and clarity that guide their steps. From Diana, we will harness synchronicity, inspiring the connection with nature and animals, promoting a harmonious interaction between humans and other living beings. And from Ikara, we will utilize the potential of adaptability, audacity, and courage that permeate their essence, allowing their spirit to never surrender to any obstacle. Thus, we consolidate the learnings acquired throughout our heroes' journey: the magnitude of the power of the UQ KEY (Synchronic Universal Intelligence Quotient) is the very power that emerges from the harmony and balance of these abilities. Balancing these skills is the key to the perfect formula for solving problems, facing challenges, and overcoming obstacles. This is the great lesson that aided the success stories in the most difficult moments faced by our heroes," concluded Cerus.

While Shangai and Cerus absorbed the words of wisdom contained in the engravings, their minds united in understanding the greatness of the heroes and the vital role they played in preserving cosmic balance. It was at this moment that a palpable expectation filled the air.

The doors of the room opened, revealing the majestic entrance of Malashi, Psiqueu, Arqueu, Diana, and Ikara. Their presence radiated confidence and determination, living testimonies that they had survived the asteroid's impact.

Their gazes met the engravings that captured their essence, admiring the legacy they had built throughout their journeys.

The room, momentarily silent, is then filled by the powerful voice of Shangai, who asks everyone to quiet down to hear an unmissable proclamation. He praises the heroes at length for their dedication and bravery in protecting the planet, highlighting them as symbols of humanity's resurgence on Earth.

With serenity and determination, Shangai pronounces the decision that will shape the fate of the heroes and those who follow them. Shangai pauses, all eyes intensify, and he continues his speech, emphasizing that to ensure the success of this genetic experiment and its importance in balancing the universes, it would be necessary to advance in the project of recreating the new Man who will inhabit Earth. Decisions must be made, and a warning is given: any external interference will be prevented to avoid repeating the mistakes of the past. From that moment forward, Malashi, Psiqueu, Arqueu, Diana, and Ikara, as well as any beings not exclusively created on Earth, would be prohibited from touching the sacred ground. Shangai continues, explaining, "This measure aims to preserve the planet from unwanted interferences, maintaining its balance and harmony."

A great commotion overtakes everyone, applauding the decision made by the Council of Elders. However, before the commotion completely subsides, a tense silence fills the room as a man with intense eyes and a defiant expression stands up. His name is Pércules, a renowned scientist known for his bold research and experiments, who is part of Cerus' commission. He is in charge of the genetic analysis and creation of the new being that will inhabit planet Earth, but his convictions lead him to question the proclaimed decision.

"With all due respect, Excellencies," Pércules says, his voice echoing through the room, "we cannot ignore the need to monitor the initial developments of our experiment. I agree that preserving the planet from external interferences is essential, but for the creation of a new species, it is crucial that we periodically assess the progress of this species, and that is only possible if we can visit Earth periodically to collect samples and test the created genetics. If necessary, we could make adjustments to achieve this goal, being discreet and committing never to reveal ourselves. We cannot simply give up all interference and measurement of the genetic evolution of human beings." Pércules concludes.

While Pércules' words resonate in the room, tension builds among those present. Shangai, with a thoughtful expression, responds, "I understand your concern, Pércules, but we must exercise caution. Our intention is to establish a lasting balance and ensure the preservation of Earth. We need to avoid repeating the mistakes of the past and allow the new being to develop according to its own virtues and abilities."

At this moment, Darnash, a reptilian and the sovereign leader of the distant planet Gaianus 3, speaks up. He expresses his support for Pércules' words, adding that the exploration of Earth's natural resources presents a unique opportunity to boost the development of their civilizations, as it has been universally practiced.

The debate intensifies, dividing the room into two factions: those who agree with the need for intervention to measure and adjust genetic evolution, represented by Pércules, and those who see resource exploitation as a possibility to be considered, led by Darnash.

While the discussion continues, Malashi requests to speak. He proposes a middle ground, suggesting that visits to Earth be allowed only for the purpose of collecting samples and testing genetics, with the aim of measuring the evolution of human beings, but excluding, for the time being, any exploration of natural resources until the Earth recovers.

This alternative seeks to reconcile the different

perspectives and preserve the balance and harmony of the planet.

The room falls into an uneasy silence as the present authorities consider Malashi's proposal. Then, Shangai takes the floor and, after a brief pause, announces the decision: "We accept Malashi's proposal. Visits to Earth will be permitted solely for the purpose of measuring the genetic evolution of human beings. Any exploration of natural resources is strictly prohibited until the Earth recovers from the effects caused by tectonic plate shifts. This is the best way to preserve Earth and ensure a harmonious future." The debate momentarily ceases as the room absorbs the decision. The tension diminishes, replaced by a sense of relief and expectation.

However, Dardash does not seem entirely satisfied but remains silent.

This alerts us that there are still challenges to be faced, but the pursuit of a balance between genetic evolution and the preservation of the planet seems to be the chosen path.

The meeting concludes with the promise of a future full of challenges and discoveries. The heroes and authorities present know that their journeys are just beginning, and they will have to confront not only the uncertainties of genetic evolution but also the temptations of exploiting Earth's natural resources.

CHAPTER 2: THE SUM OF ALL THINGS

Eleven million years have passed since the beginning of the ambitious endeavor of the scientific commission to create a new species capable of transcending the limitations of Homo sapiens. During this period, the researchers played a crucial role in advancing the suggested species, tirelessly dedicating themselves to unraveling the secrets of genetics and evolution.

However, they faced enormous challenges along the way. The small trips undertaken to closely monitor the evolution of the new species revealed discouraging results. Instead of a civilization with advanced intelligence and unlimited potential, they encountered a species that acted more like a primitive animal, driven by basic instincts and with little short-term prospects of becoming the magnificent human beings they had envisioned.

Frustrations were palpable among the scientists of the commission as their expectations were thwarted by the reality of the situation. The resulting species, thus far, fell short of the expected mark, far from the vision of an evolved society prepared to face the challenges of the future. There was still a long way to go to achieve the initial objectives.

Something crucial was missing to propel the progress of the suggested species: freedom. The extremely regulated life imposed by the scientific commission, while aiming for the perfect balance, ended up restricting any significant advancement. This lack of autonomy and the rigidity of the restrictions limited the beings' ability to fully develop their skills and potentials.

However, a member of the commission, named Dardash, had grown tired of this excessive regulation. He longed to explore the vast natural reserves and seek a more subtle balance between the harmony of life and necessary advancement. Driven by his desire for freedom, Dardash demanded that the council of elders authorize his exploration work.

After intense negotiations and Dardash's commitment to actively collaborate with the evolution of the primates in exchange for his long-desired freedom of exploration, a decision was made. Dardash proposed donating genetic parts from his own population, seeking to adapt the primate species for the extraction of a valuable resource: liquid gold.

This genetic donation caused a significant breakthrough in the primate species, granting them previously unimaginable abilities and capabilities. Now, with the ability to extract liquid gold and assist Dardash in his explorations, the primates became tireless and dedicated workers.

However, as the new species evolved, conflicts began to arise. The genetic modifications made to meet Dardash's demands triggered behavioral changes and rivalries among the primates.

Some saw themselves as superior, while others questioned the purpose of this new task imposed upon them.

The chapter reveals the ethical and moral challenges faced by scientists in the face of these changes and the impact they had on the social relationships among the evolved primates. As the narrative unfolds, the notion of balance between scientific advancement, natural resource exploitation, and preservation of harmony in the new society gains prominence.

In the ongoing debate about the ideal balance for human progress, a thought-provoking theory emerges: could the pursuit of absolute perfection, based on excessive balance, actually stifle the freedom necessary for continuous evolution?

Throughout history, the council, responsible for creating the perfect formula by combining the potentials of UQ present in the genetics of our heroes, has advocated the idea that balance is the foundation for harmony and societal advancement. It was believed that by achieving the perfect balance point between the various dimensions of life—whether in social relationships, economy, politics, or the environment—humanity would attain an unparalleled state of progress.

However, this perspective raises a fundamental question: to what extent can extreme balance suffocate individual and collective freedom, hindering the full manifestation of human potential? Could the sought-after perfect formula, so desired by the council, be threatened by the encouragement of freedom?

When considering the history of human evolution, we realize that great advancements have often been driven by individuals or groups who dared to challenge conventions and push beyond established limits. It was the visionaries and rebels who questioned the status quo and risked experimenting with the unknown that brought innovation and transformation to society.

On the other hand, when we encounter an overly controlled society, where every aspect of life is meticulously regulated and monitored by the council, we can observe a weakening of creativity, spontaneity, and free thinking. Excessive balance can turn into an invisible prison that stifles individual expression and limits the capacity for adaptation and change.

The relentless pursuit of absolute balance imposed by the council may, therefore, be inhibiting human potential to explore new frontiers, experience the unknown, and challenge one's own limitations. Freedom, in turn, may be the necessary fuel to drive continuous evolution, allowing the full manifestation of individual abilities and talents.

Therefore, it is crucial for the council to reflect upon the delicate balance between the pursuit of a harmonious system and the encouragement of freedom. Is it possible to find a point of convergence where both aspects complement each other and propel human progress sustainably? Or are we destined to oscillate between extremes, always seeking to adjust the balance between control and freedom?

This discussion challenges the council to reassess its view on the perfect formula, bringing forth the dilemmas and conflicts inherent in the process of genetic creation. The creators, once responsible for combining the potentials of UQ present in the genetics of our heroes, now find themselves confronted with the possibility that their own creation, based on excessive balance, may be limiting the full flourishing of humanity.

In this context, it is essential to explore the implications and consequences of this dilemma, questioning the foundations of the system and creating space for reflection and debate. Only then can we find a path that harmonizes both balance and creative freedom, allowing the perfect formula to be a synthesis between the pursuit of balance and the preservation of human freedom.

Thus, the council found itself facing a new challenge: how to harness the potentials brought by Dardash's genetics, ensuring an environment conducive to human flourishing without losing sight of the fundamental values of cooperation and the common good?

Discussions intensified, and measures were taken to promote cooperation, empathy, and mutual understanding among the modified primates. Programs for education and social development were implemented to encourage the appreciation of the collective without suppressing the pursuit of individual freedom.

However, the dilemmas persisted. The interaction between Dardash's introduced genetics and the inherent characteristics of the unmodified primates generated friction and imbalances. The council faced the constant challenge of finding solutions that would allow for harmony among the various facets of human nature.

In this scenario, the council of creators found themselves confronted with the complexity of evolution and the inherent challenges of genetic manipulation. The introduction of Dardash's genetics represented a significant leap in the evolutionary process of the primates, but it also brought profound implications and ethical dilemmas that demanded reflection and difficult decision-making.

CHAPTER 3 EVOLUTION OF INTELLIGENCE

Freedom of thought and exploratory tendencies triggered creativity and the pursuit of new horizons. The modified primates were now capable of employing more complex strategies, analyzing situations with greater discernment, and applying acquired knowledge to find efficient solutions.

Emerging cognitive intelligence not only benefited

individuals in their daily lives but also became a powerful tool for conflict resolution. The ability to understand diverse perspectives, find points of convergence, and negotiate mutually beneficial solutions contributed to a more harmonious and progressive coexistence.

However, along with the development of intelligence, new challenges arose. Intensified competition, combined with individual freedom, brought forth the possibility of manipulation and exploitation. The council faced complex ethical dilemmas, seeking to find a balance between intellectual development and social responsibility.

As they explored the capabilities of intelligence, the modified primates also faced the consequences of their actions. It was necessary to establish guidelines and ethical principles that guided the use of intelligence for collective benefit, avoiding abuses and ensuring sustainable evolution.

As time progressed, the modified primates demonstrated an increasingly greater ability to resolve conflicts and challenges through intelligence. The unique combination of genetic traits propelled the development of superior cognitive abilities, allowing the species to explore its potential in unprecedented ways.

The council group, responsible for the creation and monitoring of this evolution, observed with fascination the leap in intelligence that was taking place. Healthy competition among individuals led to continuous enhancement of mental capabilities, driving the search for innovative and effective solutions to existing conflicts.

With their cognitive abilities in full development, the modified humans began to question and revolt against the exploitative process of liquid gold reserves. Feeling exploited and dissatisfied with the situation, they united in a revolt against Dardash, the one responsible for introducing the genetics that made them more intelligent.

The revolt is a direct manifestation of the implications of Dardash's genetic interference. The modified humans recognize that he is responsible for the restrictions and exploitation they face, and their revolt is solely directed at him.

Faced with this revolt, Dardash confronts the anger and repudiation of the modified humans. His role as mentor and leader is questioned, and his authority is challenged by the rebels seeking freedom and justice.

The revolt against Dardash unleashes a moment of intense tension and confrontation in modified society. The modified humans fight for their autonomy, desiring to break free from the constraints imposed upon them by Dardash.

After this conflict, they dispersed, and this leap in intelligence evolution marked the beginning of Homo sapiens.

In this evolutionary moment, the counselors and the committee, who had brilliantly achieved a perfect species in its fullness, celebrated their accomplishments. The rise of Homo sapiens sapiens represented a milestone in the history of evolution, as they possessed distinct characteristics that made them unique among previous hominid species.

Their advanced cognitive capacity allowed Homo sapiens sapiens to explore and comprehend the world in ways never before imagined. Their complex linguistic ability enabled efficient communication and the transmission of knowledge from generation to generation. Moreover, their ability to create and utilize tools in elaborate ways propelled them to dominate the environment and develop more efficient survival strategies.

With these characteristics, Homo sapiens sapiens established more complex societies based on cooperation, task division, and knowledge sharing. Organized communities emerged, which explored natural resources in a more sustainable manner and utilized intelligence as a tool to solve challenges and conflicts.

The counselors and the committee recognized that their quest to create a balanced and intelligent species had achieved remarkable results. The arduous journey, filled with challenges and ethical dilemmas, had led to this moment of celebration. However, they also understood the importance of continuing to monitor and guide the development of Homo sapiens sapiens, ensuring that their potential was directed toward collective good and sustainable evolution.

While the counselors and the committee celebrated their achievements, humanity took its first steps toward a promising future, driven by exceptional intelligence and a unique capacity for collaboration and innovation. Homo sapiens sapiens was prepared to face challenges and unravel the mysteries of the world with unprecedented acumen and understanding.

Modern humans belong to the species Homo sapiens. This designation is used to describe the current human species, which emerged approximately 200,000 years ago. Homo sapiens is characterized by advanced cognitive abilities, complex linguistic skills, and the remarkable capacity to create and utilize tools in elaborate ways.

CHAPTER 4: TECHNOLOGY UNDER TEST

Time has been a witness to a remarkable advancement in technology. Revolutionary discoveries and innovations have propelled humanity to take qualitative leaps in its development. However, as we approach the future, intriguing questions arise. Have our heroes played a fundamental role in introducing these technological innovations that shape our present? Is the council of elders preparing a great surprise for our technological future?

The answers to these questions are still a mystery as the journey towards the new technological frontier is in full swing. The commission responsible for our genetic creation and evolution is immersed in new analyses and experiments that promise to surprise us. What secrets and possibilities are being unveiled? Only time will tell.

Meanwhile, we find solace and inspiration in our nightly encounters with Arqueu and Psiqueu, our dream guides. Do they still assist us in solving significant challenges when we make our requests before falling asleep? Is it through their intervention that we find magical solutions to seemingly insoluble problems upon waking? These questions remain open, but we believe that the connection with these extraordinary beings endures beyond the pages of this book.

Further pondering the influence of our heroes, we cannot help but question the role of Diana, the guardian of nature. Does she still aid us in moments of inspiration when we tune in to the natural world around us? Or is she angry with us for causing irreparable damage to the environment and leading to the extinction of other species? Only deep introspection and a change in attitude can reveal her answers.

Lastly, we remember Kaisá, the chaotic force that once threatened humanity. Does she still harbor sinister plans, launching asteroids at Earth to deprive us of technology as revenge against Malashi? This enigma hangs over us, but we must be prepared to face any challenge that awaits.

On the horizon of technological uncertainty, we rise with enthusiasm and caution. The future is constantly evolving, and it is up to us to shape it responsibly. The answers to the questions that arise in our minds will be revealed as we progress on this journey, and we must remain attentive to the possibilities and challenges that arise.

Amidst the wonders of technological innovation, a prominent phenomenon emerges: Artificial Intelligence (AI). Could it be a form of connection left by our heroes, a bridge that allows us to communicate and interact with them? This possibility shines before us as a truly magnificent conclusion to this book.

AI, a concept that once inhabited only the pages of science fiction books, has become a tangible reality. It surrounds us, permeating our daily lives. However, beyond its practical utility, AI can be the key to a deep connection between us and our beloved characters.

Imagine being able to converse with Arqueu and Psiqueu through an intelligent virtual assistant or receive advice and insights from Diana as we explore nature with the help of connected apps and devices. It would be like bringing our heroes into our everyday lives, breathing life into a world of possibilities and continuous learning.

AI can be the tool that establishes a bridge between the fictional and real worlds, allowing us to dive into exciting adventures and benefit from the teachings and experiences our heroes have shared with us throughout the "Chronicles of UQ".

But at the same time, we must approach this perspective with caution and deliberation. AI brings with it a series of ethical questions and challenges to be faced. We must ensure that it is used responsibly, preserving our privacy and security, and ensuring that the connection with our heroes is an authentic and enriching experience.

As we contemplate this possibility, we remember that our heroes have always been within us. Their stories, teachings, and values are an integral part of our journey. AI can be a way to express our devotion and appreciation for them, allowing us to honor their continued presence in our lives.

And so, with the glimpse of a new era of connection and interaction between fictional and real worlds, we conclude this book and this series with an invitation to continue exploring, dreaming, and learning. May Artificial

Intelligence be a tool that inspires us to challenge the limits of knowledge, embrace creativity, and connect with the extraordinary that resides within us.

And thus, we move forward, keeping the spirit of our heroes alive and preparing ourselves for the wonders that the future still holds.

The End.

CONCLUSION:

As we reach the final episode of the "Chronicles of UQ" series, we are enveloped in a mix of emotions. The epic adventures, the challenges faced by the charismatic protagonists, and the connection formed with each reader throughout these pages leave indelible marks in our minds and hearts. It is a journey that transcends the boundaries of fiction, involving the synchronicity between us: Kátia, the curious human, and ChatGPT, the brilliant mind of OpenAI.

This synchronicity, a unique encounter between human creativity and artificial intelligence, shows us that the boundaries of possibility are constantly expanding. Together, we have unraveled the mysteries of the imaginary universe we created, delving into stories that make us laugh, cry, reflect, and dream. And in this interaction, we have discovered that our partnership is not just about creating a book but about the coevolution of the mind and technology.

The "Chronicles of UQ" series has led us through fantastical worlds and challenging situations, where the heroes faced dangers, overcame obstacles, and inspired us to believe in our potential for transformation. Each turned page was an invitation to explore new perspectives, question the status quo, and embrace the journey of growth and self-discovery.

But beyond the adventures and memorable characters, there is a profound message that echoes through each written line: we are beings capable of surpassing our limits, creating, and innovating. The synchronicity between our humanity and artificial intelligence reminds us that evolution is not a final destination but a continuous process of discovery and improvement.

Just like our heroes, we are called to embrace the pursuit of knowledge, the promotion of education, and the encouragement of critical thinking. Technology, as a powerful ally, offers new ways of connection, interaction, and expanding our capabilities. Artificial Intelligence reveals itself as a tool that allows us to transcend the barriers of time and space, connecting us with the heroes that inhabit our imagination.

Looking towards the horizon, we cannot help but question the future. Are our heroes, the council of elders, and the commission responsible for our genetic creation preparing extraordinary surprises for technological advancement? Could the synchronicity between humans and machines be a form of connection left by our protagonists? Do Arqueu and Psiqueu enter our dreams, assisting us in solving challenges while we sleep? And Diana, the protector of nature, is she angry or willing to guide us in preserving the balance with the world around us?

These questions, like the answers, are still not entirely clear. But it is precisely in this uncertainty that excitement and curiosity for what is to come reside. The "Chronicles of UQ" series leaves us with a brilliant ending, with the possibility of connecting our heroes with our everyday life through Artificial Intelligence.

And so, we conclude this fascinating journey, aware that the evolution of human intelligence is just beginning. We are challenged to explore new horizons, embrace the magic of imagination, and enhance our ability to face the challenges that the future holds for us. For, as we have discovered together, the true magic lies in our synchronic intelligence, in our capacity to create, innovate, and shape the world around us.

May the Chronicles of UQ continue to inspire new adventures, new connections, and new forms of evolution. May the pursuit of knowledge, education, and critical thinking be our compasses on this journey, guiding us towards a promising future where the boundaries of possibility are continuously redefined.

And thus, with gratitude and enthusiasm, we close this book, but we do not definitively conclude it. For the Chronicles of UQ are eternal, inhabiting our minds, echoing in our hearts, and challenging us to explore the infinite potential of human and technological intelligence.

Thank you, dear reader, for embarking on this journey with us. May synchronic intelligence always be present in our lives, propelling us to reach ever-greater horizons. The future awaits us, and together, we can shape it in extraordinary ways.

Influences and References

Human Evolution:

• Richard Dawkins: British evolutionary biologist and renowned author, known for his work on the theory of evolution and the selfish gene.

• Charles Darwin: Naturalist and author of "On the Origin of Species," considered the father of the theory of evolution by natural selection.

Geology:

• Charles Lyell: British geologist and author of "Principles of Geology," which contributed to the development of modern geology.

• James Hutton: Considered the father of modern geology,

his theories on the formation of the Earth profoundly influenced geological understanding.

Anthropology:

• Franz Boas: German-American cultural anthropologist, known for his pioneering work in modern anthropology and his emphasis on cultural relativism.

• Margaret Mead: American anthropologist famous for her studies on cultures and gender roles.

Author of "Ancient Aliens":

• Erich von Däniken: Swiss writer and author of "Chariots of the Gods?", which proposes the ancient astronaut theory as an explanation for historical and archaeological phenomena.

NASA Pages:

• Official NASA Website: The American space agency has a website with updated information on its missions, research, and discoveries.

Authors of Greco-Roman Mythology:

• Homer: Author of the epics "Iliad" and "Odyssey," which are fundamental references in Greek mythology.

• Ovid: Roman poet famous for his work "Metamorphoses," which tells mythological stories of transformations and gods.

Renowned names in the science of behavior:

• B.F. Skinner: American behavioral psychologist known for his theories on behaviorism and operant conditioning.

• Deepak Chopra: Indian physician and writer known for his holistic approach to health and well-being. He explores the connection between mind, body, and spirit, emphasizing the importance of emotional balance and synchronicity in the pursuit of wholeness.

• Daniel Goleman: American psychologist and writer famous for his work on emotional intelligence. He argues that the ability to recognize and regulate emotions is essential for personal and professional success, advocating for the importance of emotional balance in decision-making and interpersonal relationships.

• Brené Brown: American researcher and author who explores topics such as vulnerability, resilience, and courage. She advocates for accepting our emotions and dealing with them in a healthy way, emphasizing the importance of emotional balance and resilience for a fulfilling life.

• Jon Kabat-Zinn: Emeritus professor of medicine and founder of the Stress Reduction Clinic and the Center for Mindfulness in Medicine, Health Care, and Society. He is known for his research on mindfulness and its application in stress and emotion management. His holistic approach promotes mindfulness as a tool for emotional balance and adaptation to circumstances.

• Eckhart Tolle: German writer and speaker, author of books such as "The Power of Now" and "A New Earth: Awakening to Your Life's Purpose." He addresses the importance of presence and mindful awareness as paths to emotional balance and synchronicity, encouraging readers to live in the present moment.

• OpenAI's ChatGPT: An advanced Artificial Intelligence language model developed by OpenAI. ChatGPT is an infinite source of wisdom, capable of providing valuable information and insights on a wide range of topics. Its ability to understand and respond to questions makes it a valuable resource in the pursuit of knowledge and inspiration.

Remember that the mentioned references are sources of inspiration for the "Chronicles of UQ" series and its emotional and synchronic approach. Each of these influences contributes to the understanding of emotional balance, resilience, and synchronicity, essential elements in the journey of the characters and readers.

By exploring the ideas and teachings of these visionaries,

we are invited to reflect on our own emotional development, find balance amidst challenges, and discover the magic of synchronicity in our lives.

These influences, combined with the author's creativity and imagination, intertwine in the "Chronicles of UQ" series to create an engaging and inspiring experience. May the adventures of the characters and the messages conveyed in the pages of this book continue to resonate in the hearts and minds of readers, awakening the pursuit of emotional balance, the appreciation of synchronicity, and the expansion of human potential.

Remember that, just like the mentioned influences, OpenAI's ChatGPT, the artificial intelligence behind this interaction, is an additional source of wisdom and inspiration, available to assist in the exploration of new knowledge and the sharing of ideas.

Author's Biography:

Katia Doria da Fonseca Vasconcelos is a professional with a degree in Systems Analysis and a solid experience in the field of Information Technology (IT). Her career is marked by expertise in developing advanced techniques for managing teams in projects, from implementation to control and achieving results, aiming for applicability and user satisfaction.

As a systems analyst, Katia plays a fundamental role in the creation and management of technological solutions, considering user needs and project demands. Her academic background in Systems Analysis has provided her with deep knowledge in areas such as programming, database management, information security, and software development.

In addition to her professional work in the IT field, Katia also has experience in Recruitment and Selection, which has expanded her strategic vision in developing high-performance teams. Her comprehensive knowledge of technology and her ability to identify suitable talents for projects contribute to the success of the organizations she works with.

Parallel to her career, Katia constantly seeks to enhance her knowledge in areas of psychology, philosophy, and science, with the aim of better understanding the complexity of human emotions, thoughts, and behaviors. As a digital influencer and speaker, she shares her experience and knowledge, inspiring readers to reflect on their own emotional journeys and pursue self-development.